Orangutans spend almost all of their time above the ground. They use their strong arms to swing through the trees. An orangutan has special hands and feet that are good at grabbing branches.

MONKEYS & APES

Written by Joanne Mattern

Watermill Press

Monkeys and apes are close relatives. There are 4 different kinds of apes, and about 200 different kinds of monkeys!

This orangutan is part of the ape family. Most orangutans live in hot, wet jungles.

This baby orangutan is getting a free ride! The mother lets her baby ride on her back as she travels around, looking for fruit, leaves, and insects to eat. Young orangutans stay with their mothers until they are about 7 years old.

The biggest ape is the gorilla. Gorillas are almost as tall as adult humans — and much heavier! It takes a lot of food to keep such a big body going, so gorillas spend most of their time eating plants. At night, these gentle giants sleep in the trees or on the ground.

This baby gorilla is only a few months old. When it was born, its mother carried it in her arms as she walked along looking for food. Now that it is older, the baby can ride on its mother's back.

Chimpanzees are also part of the ape family. They live in Africa. Chimps are very smart. They often use sticks to grab insects or smash fruit open with rocks. Most other animals don't know how to use tools to help them get food.

The smallest member of the ape family is the gibbon. Gibbons spend almost all of their lives in trees. They swing from branch to branch using their long, powerful arms. Gibbons often fill the air with their noisy calls. This is how these animals "talk" to each other.

This white-faced monkey is having a tasty dinner! Many monkeys eat a lot of fruit. They also eat plants and insects.

Monkeys love to play. They chase each other through the trees and watch everything going on around them.

This tiny animal is a pygmy marmoset. It is the smallest member of the monkey family. Pygmy marmosets are only about 6 inches (15 centimeters) long! They like to eat insects, spiders, and fruit.

Baboons are large monkeys. They spend most of their time on the ground. But they sometimes climb trees to find food.

Baboons like to be together. They spend a lot of time cleaning each other's fur, which is a sign of friendship.

This golden lion tamarin is one of the most unusual monkeys. It got its name because its long, orange-yellow fur reminded some people of a lion's mane. There are very few golden lion tamarins left in the wild. But you can sometimes see these colorful monkeys in zoos.

Index

Page numbers in **bold** indicate photographs.

LIBRARY OF CONGRESS CATALOGING-IN-PUBLICATION DATA
Mattern, Joanne, (date)
Monkeys & apes / by Joanne Mattern.
p. cm.
Summary: Briefly describes the four different kinds of apes and a few of the over two hundred species of monkeys found around the world.
ISBN 0-8167-2962-X (pbk.)
1. Monkeys—Juvenile literature. 2. Apes—Juvenile literature.
[1. Apes. 2. Monkeys.] II. Title. II. Title: Monkeys and apes.
QL737.P9M35 1993
599.8'2—dc20 92-28080

Printed in the United States of America.

10 9 8 7 6 5 4 3 2 1

Photo credits

Photo on page 11 © 1993 by Kim L. Weber, photo on page 13 © 1993 by Lynn M. Stone.
The following photos courtesy of Tom Stack & Associates: Photo on page 3 © 1993 by Mark Newman, pages 5 and 15 © 1993 by Larry Tackett, page 7 © 1993 by Brian Parker, page 9 © 1993 by Thomas Kitchin, page 17 © 1993 by Jack Swenson, page 19 © 1993 by Kevin Schafer & Martha Hill, page 21 © 1993 by Joe McDonald, page 23 © 1993 by Kevin Schafer.

Cover photo © 1993 by Kevin Schafer & Martha Hill/Tom Stack & Associates